Snow Toward Evening

Poems
by Melville Cane

AN ORIGINAL HARVEST BOOK

Harcourt Brace Jovanovich
New York and London

for
Jeffrey Cane Robinson

"Blood kin,
but, happier, kindred spirit."

Printed in the United States of America

Library of Congress Cataloging in Publication Data

Cane, Melville, date
Snow toward evening.

(An Original harvest book, HB 299)
I. Title.
PS3505.A557S55   811'.5'2   74-13258

ISBN 0-15-683400-6

First Harvest edition 1974
A B C D E F G H I J

Contents

These verses are chosen from four books: *So That It Flower*, 1966; *All and Sundry*, 1968; *Eloquent April*, 1971; *The First Firefly*, 1974. *So That It Flower*, the largest, represents all the poems I wished to preserve from earlier out-of-print volumes, beginning with *January Garden*, 1926.

Snow Toward Evening

Becoming a Poet

I am sometimes asked when I first took to poetry. I cannot fix even an approximate date, though I do remember, after having discovered *Palgrave's Golden Treasury* in my early teens, vaguely wishing to be represented by at least a single poem in some remotely future edition.

Nothing in my family background suggests an influence. My father's interest in the art I doubt extended beyond his high-school performance, with gestures, of Longfellow's "Excelsior." My mother, indeed, read widely in the standard authors of the day, the proper social equipment for a young maiden of the eighteen-seventies, and even translated some verses from the German. But further than this her creative impulse never stirred. I gratefully credit her, however, with stocking our non-descript shelves with one-volume editions, uncomfortable but tempting, of Burns, Scott, Moore, and Byron, and, of course, "The Complete Poetical Works" of the bearded New Englanders.

It was to these shelves that I was especially drawn almost from the very start. Unconsciously, I found growing pleasure not only in the narratives ("The Midnight Ride of Paul Revere"), but also in the sound and shape of the words as words, regardless of meaning, the interplay of vowels and consonants, the felicities of rhyme and rhythm, the metrical patterns.

It was through rhyming, I suppose, that I became originally creatively involved with the Muse, a low form of enterprise but nonetheless a beginning. Before long my doggerel—the late A. R. Orage would have termed it pupperel—found its way into the prep-school paper. Acceptance stimulated a more serious concern for craftsmanship, so that by the time I entered Columbia College as a freshman I was on the way to qualifying as a light-verse practitioner in good standing. Incidentally, I even acquired a professional status, not as a jongleur, but as a concocter of jingles.

One day a manufacturer of watches and clocks wrote to the president of Columbia University asking him to recommend a student "confident to write poetry." He handed the letter to his secretary for attention. The secretary, Frederick Paul Keppel, ultimately president of the Carnegie Corporation, and a good friend, showed me the letter and inquired whether I felt "confident." I said I did, and, after a satisfactory interview with the merchant, produced a jingle for each page of his annual catalogue illustrating the latest designs in timepieces. Payment: fifty dollars. My work must have proved invaluable to the business, since it at once achieved a rapid growth under the name of Longines Wittnauer Watch Company.

My second (and only other) commercial job was for Wallach's Laundry, a concern I think no longer exists. The task was to publicize in verse the virtues of Wallach's over those of all competitors in the trade. This I contrived, despite the handicap of a prosaic theme, in a series of quatrains which placarded the streetcars of the city for a long time. Though well paid, I derived the main satisfaction from reading the printed placards as I rode about town.

Aside from these two assignments, from my junior year on, in addition to contributions to the Columbia magazines, I began to send verse to the periodicals whose acceptances were accompanied with pay checks. These included the national weeklies *Puck, Judge,* and the old *Life,* and the more genteel monthlies *Harper's,* the *Century,* and *Leslie's.* To the former went my more knockabout pieces, to the latter the strict, formal compositions, usually *vers de société* in the manner, then prevalent, of the Englishmen Charles Stuart Calverley, Frederick Locker-Lampson, and Austin Dobson.

I recall an incident of that period the value of which was not brought home to me for twenty-odd years. One day I ventured to send a few of my Dobsonish poems to *Punch.* Instead of the usual impersonal rejection slip, they were returned with what should have proved a helpful letter. In substance, the editor pointed out that he was not passing on the merits of the submissions, but, rather, on the fact that they were of the same variety as those he was receiving, overplentifully, from his British contributors. Why, he earnestly ended, did I not write as an American? It was American verse he would be most happy to consider.

But this excellent advice went unheeded. I was too immature and timid to develop a poetic personality of my own.

The first intimation of such a remote possibility came unexpectedly one December night in 1899. I stood on the open Columbia campus late in the evening; the life and confusion of the city below Morningside Heights receded as I surrendered to the splendor of a cosmic spectacle. In a state of elation I hastened home to record the experience before it evaporated. The brief poem, which I called "Winter Night," follows:

> Winter-cold is the night.
> Chiseled in deepest blue,
> Each star-shape silver-white
> Shines cold-clear down the sky's long avenue.
> The rich moon with its broadly streaming flood
> Washes with light
> The earth whereon I stand.
> The icy ether fires my smouldering blood,
> The stars I breathe and feel,
> The magic heavens my trembling senses steal,
> Until, exquisitely unmanned,
> My spirits swoon
> With the delicious cold, the dark, the riding moon.

Next day I showed it, hesitantly, to Professor George Edward Woodberry, himself a poet. He read it slowly, silently, as I waited for the verdict. He read it several times. Finally, in a single sentence, came these words: "Boy, this is the real thing."

And then he proceeded to note the particulars in which I had in his opinion succeeded, especially a Keatsian richness of atmospheric detail and an honesty in reporting the experience. A devotee of Shelley, praise from him carried added weight.

With the approach of graduation from Columbia College loomed the troublesome prospect of choosing a career. In this, my twentieth year, I lived enjoyably absorbed in the present, ill prepared to make a mature commitment that might govern the future course of life. Furthermore, aside from the writing of poetry, I possessed no special bent, no enthusiasm or predilection, no singleness of drive or of purpose strong enough to simplify a solution of the problem.

Any decision necessarily had to be realistic and its consequences foreseeable. As the year went by, two alternatives began to take shape: journalism and law. As for journalism, I had gained apprentice experience by working on the college papers as both reporter and editorial writer, and had sent an occasional news story to one of the city dailies.

The practice of law, on the other hand, seemed less inviting; in fact, the very consideration of law as a livelihood arose from a set of factors, if not contrary to my nature, at least with no apparent relation to it. The factors were both sentimental and economic. The sentimental appeal arose out of a parental ambition, especially common, supposedly, among the Jews, to have at least one "professional man" in the family, a representative who would function on sublimer heights than those of mere commerce. In our case such a representative was to have been my Uncle Abe, who had started out to become a lawyer, only to end up in the clothing business. It was but natural that the family should turn to me, a generation later, to make good where he had failed them.

More cogent, however, was the economic factor, the need for financial security in some suitable field that promised a decent living. The uncertain state of our own affairs at the moment most certainly colored, or clouded, the question. My father's business, which was the manufacture of boys' clothing, seemed to run a broken course of seasonal ups and downs; we were alternatively prosperous or on the edge of trouble. Right then the weather looked unsettled.

In all fairness, it should be recorded that the suggestion of law as a vocation was never pressed upon me by the family in any coercive manner. It was presented simply for my consideration. More persuasive and determinative counsel came from Professor Woodberry. In every sense a distinguished, well-published man of letters in the fields of biography, literary criticism, and poetry, he had never received from his books a steady competence, but was required to turn to teaching and lecturing for a more dependable return. So, after having heard my story, he reluctantly favored caution rather than daring.

In the fall of 1900 I entered the Columbia Law School.

My three-year stretch would have rated dismally low in any aptitude test. (Unconsciously, I have used the word "stretch," a prison term.) Despite conscientious effort, for I was regular in class attendance and had sharply cut down outside activities, including writing, I fought a losing though uphill struggle with the material. In vain I searched for the causes of my bewilderment and failures. Why did I flunk two courses the first year and three at the end of the second year, when my friends passed each time with comparative ease? In the Columbia Law School of today, I would never have been tolerated to muddle on, but would have been chucked out after the first year.

Nonetheless, the discouraging experience did pay unexpected dividends, to be cashed in at some distant date. As a change from classroom tensions I turned to journalism and spent three humid law-school summers, first, on the *Commercial Advertiser,* then on the *Evening Post,* and, in 1903, on the *Globe.* Through the variety of my assignments, which included a two weeks' coverage of Police Headquarters and a sensational murder trial in Brooklyn, I acquired firm professional status plus a living wage as a reporter. Better still, I gained sufficient self-confidence to consider newspaper work as a future calling should the law school turn me down.

Summer vacations were necessarily skimpy, and were followed in early September by a bone-up period to prepare for re-examinations in the subjects I'd been deficient in. Surprisingly, I cleared the slate each time. I received my LL.B. degree, and, after one unsuccessful try, was admitted to practice in 1903.

The story of my career as a lawyer requires a separate chapter unwritten to date. It need only be said here that the challenge to make good in a profession to which I was not well suited commanded and consumed all of my resources for many years.

It is enough to record my deep satisfaction on receiving in 1948 the Columbia University Medal for Excellence, which, according to the citation, recognized my work both as lawyer and as poet.

Meanwhile, as a writer of light verse I coasted along on the old level, publishing for the most part in Franklin P. Adams' columns as they appeared, first in the *Mail and Express* and later in the *World, Herald Tribune,* and *Post.*

The conviction, however vague, that I might some day be able to tap deeper creative sources persisted alongside the suppressive frustrations induced by a total involvement in the law. I still retained the memory of my "Winter Night" poem as a sign, though slight, of a genuine, personal expression, and I carried with that memory the assuring critical respect of Mr. Woodberry. Parenthetically, it should be added that throughout these trying years my "literary" side was nourished and sustained by reading the new poets and the current criticism.

These frail supports could not overcome a mounting sense of insufficiency, of a life only half lived, with corresponding discontent and unhappiness in my professional confinement and in my personal relations. Finally, the conflict became so acute, destructive, and uncontrollable that I turned to psychoanalysis for light and hoped-for relief. I need only report that the ensuing rapport gradually loosened the adhesions to conforming habit, opened the sealed chambers of the unconscious, until I produced a solitary poem out of deep inner experience, quite definitely a personal expression. What added to the miracle, for so I regarded it, was the contrast it presented to the aesthetic values of my youth; in those silent, seemingly fruitless years a transition beneath the surface had been slowly in the making. From a Victorian, pro-Tennysonian position I now found myself open to the fresh currents of the poetic renaissance of the nineteen-twenties. A few more pieces followed the initial breakthrough. For a while I withheld them from publication, in order to make sure they were not flashes in the pan but were moving along firm ground.

At last came the fateful test, a submission to the *Dial.* The poem was "January Garden," somber, loosely, not completely, rhymed, with a new-found freedom. It pleased the editors to take it, wrote Miss Alyse Gregory, and would I kindly send on a brief biographical note to go with the poem?

I had arrived! at least for the moment. And, what counted more, I had "made" the most distinguished avant-garde magazine of the day. Succeeding Miss Gregory as editor, Miss

Marianne Moore followed her example and took four more of my poems in the years to come.

With this impressive recognition I grew more positive, readier to accept myself as a poet and to regard the practice of poetry as the basic indispensable of my life. That year, 1925, by an unprecedented act of independence, I abandoned the family for a truancy at Ogunquit, Maine, where, alone, by the end of a month's uninterrupted concentration I emerged with a small body of work I was not ashamed to stand behind. I dared think in terms of a book, and sent the batch to Donald Brace. I still cherish his letter saying that the firm of Harcourt, Brace and Company "would be proud to publish." The title of the book was *January Garden*.

When did I first take to poetry? was the question in the first sentence of this paper. Not so long ago, an incident occurred that not only throws light on a moment in time, but also reveals me to myself as of that same moment, the way a forgotten but rediscovered snapshot may do years later. One Sunday morning while I was walking along Park Avenue an elderly man approached and stopped short in front of me. "Aren't you Mel Cane?" he asked, and I admitted I was. "I'm Dave Myers," he went on. "We were in the same class at P.S. 70 on East Seventy-fifth Street." Then he said reminiscently: "On Friday afternoons—remember?—there were no set classes; we could do whatever we felt like. Most of us would play games in the yard, but you used to stick indoors and read poetry. 'The murmuring pines and the hemlocks.' " He smiled as he moved away, and I smiled back.

A further bit of self-revelation, more significant in throwing light on my early dedication, appears in a lately found letter written when I was eighteen to my chum and classmate Alfred Cohn. It contains the following outburst, quite uncharacteristic of the light, unemotional tone of my customary letters:

". . . I often feel as if I wished to write a really serious poem, in fact, I started one—perhaps it will appear ridiculous in your eyes—so uncertain am I of the result. You see, if I ever shall have any literary future and God knows I'm earnest and industrious enough, this is the time to experiment and to 'feel,' as Mr. Kipling has been doing according to last January's 'Bookman,' 'for the spring which when touched will disclose the hidden secret of his nature.' I am trying to find myself, as the saying is. I'm glad that I wrote this letter because it's a long time since I've been able to open my heart, or to be on speaking terms with myself."

Reflecting on influences that may have affected my work I know that both law and literature have contributed importantly. In matters of technique and craftsmanship, the Imagist approach proved especially serviceable, because it replaced laxity in describing an object or scene with insistence on a refining, heightened accuracy, a sharper sensuous awareness. Beyond this technical contribution, however, I parted company with the Imagists, whose productions seemed for the most part static, lacking those overtones that cause a poem to linger on and become memorable.

The law, too, had even more to offer. From years of experience in drawing contracts, affidavits, and legal briefs I learned the discipline of conciseness and brevity of statement. This discipline I adopt when composing lyrics; they gain, I believe, in their impact through succinctness. My narrative poems, of course, proceed from the opposite approach, running to length, with a tempo more suited to the telling of a tale.

Naturally I had and have my favorite poets; a study of their subject matter and their craftsmanship suggest new points of view, new techniques I might consider if not adopt. As I change, for better or worse, my favorites also change. For example, an earlier enthusiasm for *The Shropshire Lad,* with its impeccably rhymed stanzas, waned as later I grew more conscious of their monotonous pessimism. On the contrary, the verses of Hardy, often less perfect in form, grow more meaningful, particularly in their wider outlook over the human scene. To make a general observation requiring infinite modifications: in the beginning my interest ran first to word play, to manner, to form; now, with no sacrifice of these values, I increasingly look toward the matter, the substance.

I remember the suggestive comments of Professor Woodberry after he had read *January Garden.* "Your verses are unicellular," he wrote, "and alright, as far as they go; they remind me of delicate watercolors." Of course he was right, even charitable, in his limited approval of these first feeble steps.

A few weeks after *January Garden* appeared in early June of 1926, my wife and I planned a European trip, my first. When I announced this to my analyst, she hesitated as if in thought, then suddenly came out with this unbelievable proposal: "Would you care to meet Dr. Jung?" The question required no answer, I was so overwhelmed. "But don't for a moment count on it," she went on more cautiously. "At most there's only an off-chance. You see, it will be the end of his season when you get over, his busiest time, and he always shuts up shop promptly on July 15th, to leave for his summer vacation at Bollingen, farther up the lake. I'll write him where he can reach you, if you'll give me your Paris address. But I say again, don't count on it."

A few days later we took ship and soon after were absorbed in sight-seeing. We had barely settled down to a tourist routine when a phone call from the Guaranty Trust Company said that there was a telegram for me. Our first reaction was one of alarm; some accident might have occurred to one of the children. The message, however, proved of quite a different nature. It read: "Can see you to-morrow evening seven o'clock, Küsnacht; have reserved room Hotel Bauer-au-lac, Zurich. Wire answer. Signed Carl Jung."

Were ever plans more fortunately upset?

I did promptly wire, quickly arranged for my wife to stay with friends, and within hours boarded a Wagon-Lit for the night trip, which would land me at Zurich next morning.

How I contrived to kill the hours of that overlong day of waiting remains vague. Stunned and tense with anticipation I wandered aimlessly about the city in no mood for cultural things. I remember sitting on a bench at the approach to the Zurichsee, watching the passing scene and having a hasty snack on my way to the railroad station for Küsnacht. A short trip and a short walk along Seestrasse brought me to the gate I was looking for. As I opened it the master of the house, puffing his after-dinner pipe, strode down the garden path to greet me. I recall the warmth of his handshake, the simple words of welcome—in unlabored English, to my relief—as he led me through the house to his study. Soon my self-consciousness wore off under the spell of his personality, for he guided the conversation as an exchange between friends. That swift hour bore little resemblance to any professional office visit.

As I stood to leave and thank him I felt we were at home with each other. He noticed a book in my hand; it was a copy of *January Garden* I had meant to give him, but had almost forgotten to. He took it, then quite simply asked: "Would you like to call again?" As I nodded, he said: "How about tomorrow morning at eight?"

At eight o'clock I was again at his gate, and again, as on the previous evening, he had noticed my approach and was walking toward me, this time with book in hand. "Good morning," he briefly said, and then: "I have read your book. You are a true poet!"

I cannot exaggerate or overrate the impact of these few precious words; they enveloped me with a current of new-found strength; they infused fresh hope after months of creative futility and sterility. Dramatically they supplied an element completely lacking in my prior analysis, for my poems had never been examined in terms of art, but merely as material drawn from the unconscious, to be interpreted within that psychological framework. Dr. Jung had indeed made an aesthetic judgment, but it was more than that in the effect it produced. I felt it as a blessing bestowed not so much for the meager accomplishment, but also as a gift to be earned in the process of time.

During my two weeks' stay at Küsnacht, besides almost daily sessions, I was invited by Dr. and Mrs. Jung to many social gatherings. In each case, with uncanny diagnostic sense Dr. Jung would introduce me as "an American poet" and never as a New York lawyer.

All this happened a half century ago, but to this very day the uncertain contest goes on, with its unpredictable alternations of light and darkness, its dread of the day the perverse stream might trickle off, to stifle in sand.

The plight of the poet was truly expressed by the British poet

C. Day Lewis, in these few words: "The Muse, though she visit her poet fitfully, is the ground of his being. She will not come meekly to his call."

This statement I have expanded into these lines:

> She'll visit him but fitfully,
> Not meekly to his call;
> He dare not chide demandingly
> (She owes him nothing rightfully);
> He first must serve her faithfully
> And painfully, yet gratefully,
> To gain her favor—possibly,
> Or else lose all.

Whatever the motive, and there are many that lead to the writing of verse, it always stems, I believe, from the need to make a concrete design out of unexpressed feelings, sensations, intuitions, to extract particles of order out of the general chaos.

In support of this belief I submit the following poem to suggest at least one of the elements involved in the process of creation:

Minutiae

The precise split second when the tide turns,
The degree of pain between a twitch and a twinge,
The hairline between the just-too-much and the not-quite-
                                                            enough,

The exact telegraphy and registry of intuitions,
The refinement of the cloudy general into its luminous
                                                            particulars—

Each fresh discovery of sleeping differences,
Each shade and grade and tint,
Each new and sharp nuance,
Each hard-won nicety,
Rejecting the merely approximate,
The short-of-accurate,
The too-readily-acceptable—

All these
(Momentous minutiae!),
So dear to man's concern.

To refine "the cloudy general into its luminous particulars";
to seek the enlargement and deepening of consciousness, the
human fulfillment, the divine illumination!

To Build a Fire

The hearth waits,
Clean and bare and ready.

First:
To lay the paper,
A bed of prose to start with.

Then:
Artfully, bit by bit,
Add shavings,
Curling phrases,
Kindling symbols.

Contrive a rhythmic nest of sticks
And crown it with symmetric logs.

Finally:
Loosen and unclog,
That air may flow
And flame may catch.

The Pencil

Loose in the hand,
Inanimate,
A pencil lies in wait
For his command,
A humble conduit,
Obedient to transmit
Whatever's given it.

Whatever shall that be?
Who knows the chemistry
Of rage or ecstasy?

A current startles the heart,
Darts a quickening signal
To the fingers,
Enters the instrument,
A mounting song along a dark canal.

The tunneled miracle
Funnels to the light,
Luminous on the blank white page.

Radiance transmutes the livid lead
To living blood.

Behind Dark Spaces

Somewhere, behind dark spaces,
Light races.
Pressure
Of rushing light
Tears a fissure
Across night,
A crack
In black less black.

Gradual starry withdrawal,
Cool of sky's vague pool,
Faint disclosure of rose,
Blue palely filtering through,
Under grim black, dim
Earth-green,—
Emerging scene.

Out of shreds, out of seeds, of utter gray,
Ultimate, brightly-woven, high-flowering day.

Petition

To be still
As a hill,
To be cool
As a pool,
To dare
To be bare,—
To be nil;

To surrender the will
That the will may be free
To submit, as the sand to the sea;

That the hope
May take shape,
As the sand from the sea;

That the dream,
No longer a dream,
Shall finally be;

That the soul
Shall be earthless,
Earthless and whole.

At This Unlikely Hour

Embers crumble
Mauve to ashen,
Dust of passion
Snows the hearth.

Now the hearth's a grave,
Save for an unsuspected spark
That lurks and circumvents the dark,
And bursts to flower
At this unlikely hour.

The Task

How to cope
With the flight of hope;

Under despair
How to endure,
(Endure! Endure!)

And be more than a leaf
On the gale of grief,

And perceive, as only a fraction,
The pain and distraction.

How, in the perilous instant,
To hold, how feebly, the constant;

How feebly,
The way, the meaning, the mystery.

How, in the clutch of extinction,
Still to function, human!

This is the task, the prayer,—that I may save
The suffering god within, that he may live,
And greatly live, beyond the grave.

So That It Flower

To heed the flash and speed the leap
Out of the dark, designless deep,
And shield the intrinsic, undefined,
From the perversions of the mind,
And warm the seed with sacred care,
And nurse the seed with love and prayer
So that it flower, pure and fair.

A Man from Porlock

In the midst of recording KUBLA KHAN, which had come to him complete in a dream, Coleridge was interrupted by a visitor, "a person on business from Porlock." The intrusion broke the spell; "all the rest had passed away like the images on the surface of a stream into which a stone has been cast."

He dreams and breathes an ether rarer
Than natural air, of splendor fairer
Than planet-blaze, distilled of honey-dew,
Gilding the pleasure-dome of Xanadu;

And journeys on through fabulous dimensions
Of time and space, to measureless expansions,
Tracing the mystic venture of the soul
Along its bright and labyrinthine trail.

A blessed region, a celestial season,
A realm where magic rules and outlaws reason,
A poet's universe of song and sight,
Of ecstasy and radiance and delight;

An atmosphere too exquisite, too pure
To mix with cruder substance and endure.

Whether a man from Porlock or our own
Unbidden daemon casts the crucial stone,
The end's the same: the most we can redeem
Is but a fragment of the dream.

Two Stars

Two stars lie caught in a tree.

A shriveling angle
Of sight,—that snares a star in a tangle
Of leaves,—that shrinks a star to a spangle!

I have only to stand, to free them,
To step three steps, to see them
Clear of earth and true to sky,
Eye to eye.

Two stars rose from a tree.

Humbly, Wildly

Water boils on the flame,
For use, for need;
Water boils in the flume,
A torrent freed.
Element bound in a pot,
Humbly to serve;
Current of passion untamed,
Crashing to curve.

Such, the Simple Meaning

Sun is hidden; veils of gray
Drift and gather round the bay,
Dimming from view
The last thin patch of sky
Drained of blue.

Tide keeps running out to the cry
Of gulls zig-zagging, calling shrill and dry.
A tiny yellow bird over and over
Pecks at delectable clover.
Like a snail
A vague tanker smears a smoky trail.

Fine rain sifts a bloom on the spruces,
Gently reduces
Pearly distance,
Blurs the cliff of terra cotta,
Dulls the light-house, squat
Upon the headland,—
Shapes a deeper bay, screening
Me from outward circumstance.

Such, the simple meaning.

Night at Noon

The early morning sparkle disappeared
With the blue; by noon the sun was blurred.
Lower, ever lower,
The sinister and leaden
Element extended, ever making duller
The meager residue of color.
Nothing remained to deaden.
It seemed the end of day, of life,—the end.
Then as the final moment of despair
Let down a subtle weight upon the air,
Its ruthless pressure forced a feeble stir;
The stir persisted, struggled to defend
Its dubious motion, spread to the inner
Reaches of the dark. The pall grew thinner,
Reluctantly withdrew
Within itself. No hidden sun pressed through.
And yet, though imperceptible to sight,
One grew aware it was no longer night.

A Harvest to Seduce

Upon the tree of time
The fruit looms high,
The fruit so fair to pluck!
The hour's late and black.
The time-tree quivers,
Loosens and delivers
The midnight crop.

Twelve drop,
A harvest to seduce,
Lacking joy or juice.

Beware the vain lament,
The hunger for what's spent.
This is dead-sea fruit
And ashes to the taste.
Quash it with your foot.
What is past is past.

Country-House: Midnight

The key of the lamp clicks,
And as it locks the light
The full black tide rolls in.

This had been a room,—
Warm wing-chair,
Peacocks strutting over chintz,
Blake's "Job,"
Telephone.

Black now floods the human spaces,
Drenches the hearth,
Topples every shape to shapelessness.

High, where a clock companionably sat,
A metal rat's-tooth
Evenly nicks and nibbles.

Rural Dumpheap

This rusty mound of cans,
This scatter of tires and pans,
This litter of mattresses and twisted springs,
This rotting refuse, these abandoned things
Malodorously flung,—this impudent pile
That dares to choke the current, to defile
The innocent season,—all are man's.

Man's inhumanity to sod
Makes countless snow-drops mourn,
And every gentle seed that's born
Gives battle for a dishonored god.

Within the heap and darkly, heaves
The growing mutiny of leaves,
While down the valley bird to bird
Relays the rallying word,
And courage calls on every breeze
To armies of anemones,
And triumph scales the parapet,
A host of violet.

O man, where is thy victory?
Despite this blight of tins,
The fern persists and cleaves and wins,
And, gladly, spring begins.

Feelings

The cat killed a rat.
Magnificent in conquest
It lay basking.
How splendid the cat!
How horrid, how venomous the rat!
I breathed heavy with exultation
Over my enemy
Stiff and ugly in the dust.

It was no rat;
It was a baby rabbit,
Warmness running out.
Tender, curving back!
Soft, pathetic fur!
Innocent, wondering eyes!

The proud cat crumples and slinks,
Wind rips the roses,
A cloud bags the sun.

Many Races Have I Run

Many races have I run
With fate and fate has always won.

Often less than by the inch
Of an intuition's flinch;

Often less than by the flash
Signaling: "Faith will crash!"

Often less than can be reckoned
By what
Is but an inert spot
Within a second.

But most
I've lost
By the same mischance—
One back glance.

An Hour Ago

An hour ago the sky seemed permanent blue,
No sign could show
From what destructive roots these storm-winds grew
Or why these black rains flow.

An hour ago the sea was gentle as death,—
What smoldering cause
Inflamed these foamy fangs, this poisonous breath,
These clinching claws?

An hour ago my heart was shaken with pain;
I know not how
It came or ceased, or what may happen again
An hour from now.

End of Daylight-Saving

When I was rich in April
They robbed me of an hour,
But, having many, many,
It was plucking one flower,
Or stealing one penny.

Brooks poured fast,
Flowers pushed thickly,
Hours slid past,—
All too quickly.

But brooks drain thin,
Flowers dry seedy,
Light draws in,
Now I'm needy.

The thief must have learned it
And, giving no warning,
Mysteriously returned it
One crisp morning.

When I was rich in April
Before the early leaves,
Long before this ditty,
I never thought of thieves,
Or that thieves felt pity.

A Rat

There's a rat in the wall,
A rat in the wall,
At the side of the bed
Close to the head;
Gnawing a path
Through a thicket of lath,
Pawing a track
Through a forest of black.

Will it nibble and scratch
Till it loosens the latch
Of the portal of me?—
Will it scrape itself free?
Will it crumble and master
The wavering plaster
That leans between me and disaster?

Dawn Has Yet to Ripple In

What is this that I have heard?
Scurrying rat or stirring bird?
Scratching in the wall of sleep?
Twitching on the eaves of sleep?
I can hear it working close
Through a space along the house,
Through a space obscure and thin.
Night is swiftly running out,
Dawn has yet to ripple in,
Dawn has yet to clear the doubt,
Rat within or bird without.

Hymn to Night

Now it grows dark.
Red goes
Out of the rose;
Out of the lawn
Green's withdrawn;
Each buttercup now yields
Its gold from blurring fields;
Larkspur and sky surrender
Blue wonder.

We were dark within, we relied
For our strength on the nourishing sun;
Now it is under and gone.
Now, as the light grows duller,
We, who had flourished on color,
Stand, in the ever-deepening shade,
Bereft, dismayed.

We were dark within, it was death
We saw, we had never seen
Within the dark, we had never known
The spark, the vital breath.
If only we had known
That black is neither loss nor lack
But holds the essential seed
Of mortal hope and need!

Now sheltering dusk,
Shepherd of color and light for dawns unending,
Tends the holy task.

Praise be to black, the benign,
No longer malign,
Prolonger of days!
Praise the preserver of shine,
The keeper of blaze!

Praise Night,
Forever praise
Savior Night,
Who surely stays
The arm of time,
Who guards the flame,
Who hoards the light.

Praised be the Night.

I Remember Distinctly

I remember distinctly the time, when I said
To myself, as the thought,
Unsought,
Flashed through my head:
"Some day I shall see you no more;—
You will be dead."

I remember distinctly the place,
Where I said, face to face
With myself: "Some
Day it will come, it will come;
The dread summons will come."

And I said I must waste
No time,—there is not a moment to waste,
To school the heart for its burden,
To harden
The frail, irresolute will.

And I labored, I built, until
I fancied the imminent blow
As a scattering, impotent blow
Against a texture, toughened and tuned
To any threatened wound.

But out of the black
A thunder crack!
The will is riven,
The heart cloven.

On Barren Rocks I Poured
My Blood

On barren rocks I poured my blood
And where I stood,
Before my clouded eyes
And under desolate skies
A miracle occurred.
Something stirred!
And over the changing planet
Flowers dared the peril
Of regions sterile,
And grasses pierced the granite.

Gulls

Gulls, you are so absurd!
Only a moment ago,
Poised along that sandy, glistening bar,
You seemed to be settling down till the tide should cover.
Now
Bits of snow-white paper in a storm
Sprinkle Heaven with chaotic flight.
Why this silly hysteria
That rips the sky with schoolgirl giggle and gabble?

Futile zigzags,
Broken spirals,
Drooping glide to soothing mud.
Refreshed, you rise and repeat,
You sink and repeat.

What is the true diagnosis
Of your ornithological neurosis?

I watch you whirl in white superb delirium
Against the deep-green density of pines.
Can it be
That you revolve in some mysterious rhythm
Beyond the earth-bound logic of my senses?
That your ecstatic unreason,
Your baffling disorderly beauty
An infinitesimal point may mark
On some wider arc?
And that your wild cacophonies
May sound a pure harmonious phrase
In a music of infinite rapture
That I have yet to capture?

Death

It is sweet, toward the end of day,
To step, out of the roar,
Out of the glare,
Into the room, it is still,
Into the flooding final light;
Sweet, as the noises fade,
As the pressure lifts,
To be wrapped in the warmth of the sun,
To be cradled gently in sleep.

Bruised but intact,
Sound in retreat,
I have slipped from the pitiless city
To the peace of the room,
The harbor of light,
The shelter of sleep.

Clear of pursuit,
Weary of flight,
I have fallen asleep in the ebbing sun;
Deeply,
With even breath,
I have sunk in the sea of the dark,—
Like a child, I have lain on the breast of the dark,
To awake,
To arise,
In a world of stars.

Houdini

The papers said:
"Houdini Dead!"
Racing newsboys yelled:
"Houdini dead! Houdini dead!"
People read, smiled:
"Just another front
Page publicity stunt."
But Houdini was dead.

How can one get away with it,—
The box-trick,—
How can one fool Death?

No one could fix the committee,
An undertaker, chairman.
Dead men play no tricks,
But was he "playing dead"?
How could a dead magician
Put it over a live mortician?

They clamped him with manacles,
Shackled his ankles,
Clapped him in a case,
Strapped him to his place,
Locked the lid.
He did what he was bid.
They kept the watch by day,
They vigiled him by night
In the sputtering candle-light.
He never left their sight.

They bore him from the house,
They caged him in a hearse
(The hearse was framed in glass,
Was screwed with screws of brass,
And only light could pass).

They took him for a ride,
Captive, chained and tied;
They set him on the ground,
Coffined, fettered, bound,—
The damp November ground.
He made no sound.

The grave was dark and deep,
The walls were high and steep;
They lifted him and lowered him,
They shoveled earth, a heavy heap—
A rising heap, a dwindling hole.
A rabbi made a prayer for his soul.

II

Years ago, a mid-summer day,
Saugatuck, Long Island Sound.
Suddenly he stepped out on the shore,
Dropped his robe,
A bather,
Smiling, bowing, in the sun.
Incredulous ones
Peered within a packing case,
Felt for secret panels,
Tapped each side.
Strangers tied him, hand and foot and torse,
Hammered fast the top with nails of steel,
Roped and double-roped and tugged the knots.
A high derrick dipped,
An iron hook slipped,
Clinched the rope,
Pulled its dangling burden clear of land,
Plunged it in the waves.
Then, as it rose again, a swinging minute,
A swimmer stroked his triumph toward the bank.

To do the box-trick in water,
When the July sun is shining,

Is hard;
But, harder still,
On a cold November day
To swim through clay.

III

This was no mountebank,
No spangled juggler
Of rubber-balls and billiard cues and lamps—
This was and is and ever will be spirit.
There is a legerdemain
Unsensed by mortal fingers,
A clairvoyance
The perishable brain
Is hopeless to attain.
There is a heart-beat of the spirit;
No one can time it.
There is a blood, a muscle, of the soul.
Lithe is the spirit and nimble
To loose the cords of the body;
Wiry and supple the soul
To slip the strait-jacket of the flesh.

IV

Out of an unbroken grave,
Above unheeding mourners,
Before the sightless eyes of conjurors,
Houdini rose
And lightly sprinted down an aisle of air
Amid the relieved and welcoming applause
Of those already there.

Each to Each

We were closed, each to each, yet dear.
We were taut with a covert pride;
We were tied
With a throttling fear;
We were undefined
And blind.

We were caught when we sought to reach;
We were mute when we strove for speech.
We were closed, each to each, yet dear.
We were vapid, polite, obscure
Through a merciless flood of pain;
We were trivial through strain;
We were desperate to endure.

Then a locked word slipped from your heart,
Like warm rain dropped on mine,
And the fog that had held us apart
Thinned,—we could dimly divine
The one we had groped for in vain.

And my hand touched yours, and the pain
That clutched and withered had fled,
And the fear and the pride lay dead,
And at last we were free, we were plain.

We were closed, each to each, yet dear.
We are close; we are clear.

All I Knew

There was no reason, no warning;
All I knew—you were there!
As infallibly there
As the crystal air
That April morning.

There was no hint or suggestion
Of person or past;
I moved alone, serene in a vast
Non-human scheme, in a harmony cast
Too right for question.

I was one with the rising season,
With April's every leaf and earliest bud;
April's crystal flood
Sent a new fire streaming in the blood.
No warning, no reason!

Octagons and Roses

Since I prefer octagonals to circles,
And since I crave the odor and color of roses,
May I, therefore, lop their curves,
Square their petals?
Roses have rights,
I, desire.
Should I mutilate the rose
I should violate desire.
One should seek elsewhere for octagonals.

I Have Heard

I have heard
The arrested cadences of bells
When bells no longer sway;
I have found
The sound that swells from silence,
That dwells and drifts in silence following sound;
I have known
The melody
That dies in throats of birds.

And now, at last, I hear
The call you never voiced, I never answered,
Now you have ceased to call.

It Digs a Double Grave

Your pain
Is a weight of stone
Upon my heart; your pain
Is mine.

Your pitiful eyes entreat,
Your lips beseech;
Our eyes, our lips, meet
In silent speech;
We are one,
Under your pain.

But love is less than love
That cannot give or save,
And when love closely cleaves
To that for which it grieves
It digs a double grave.

To part you from your pain,
To set you free,
I must myself be free
Or else be slain.
Loving, detached, still,
I must call on brain and will
Ever to cool and steel
This heart, too eager, lest it overfeel.
Then, only, can I heal.

Give Way to Grief

Give way to grief,
And, unashamed,
Abandon stoic fortitude a while.
Set free a while, the soul,
Better to bear its load.

Tears unshed are stones upon the heart
That choke the healing stream.

Unlock the flood-gates;
Loose the waters.
Give way, and cope with grief.

Within the Dark

I search to find you in the shining day.
In vain.
This shallow radiance
Advances merely to the outer eye,
Reveals no deeper than the natural scene
Of earth to sky
And then lets down its screen.

Beneath, behind,
My vision fails
(Your vision veiled)
And I'm undone and blind.

Now darkness spreads and swells the dark within.
I close the door and move across the room
You brightened once, now tenanted by gloom.
Oh, dare I hope that what has been
May come to pass again!

I draw the curtains, strike a flickering match,
Linger before the fireplace,
Wait for the wood to catch,
Invoke the gradual flame, the missing face.

I seek a light that lies beyond the sun,
(Nor here, within this fire) a sacred source
That emanates from blackness and that runs
Along no earthbound course.

The embers sag, the rose dissolves to ash,
The hovering darkness deepens and surrounds,
And I am stayed and heartened by the hush,
The gathering calm, the quietude profound.

Beneath this calm a hidden current stirs;
A faint, insistent rumor on the night,
Whispers of memory, a messenger's
Annunciation heralded in light.

The rumor grows; I reconstruct the scene:
Your final presence here, the season, late
October, golden-leaved; our world serene.
We sat, as I do now, before the grate,

The room unlit, as now, the fading glow
Defining, as it spread, your shadowy form.
Your hand reached mine; we were contented so;
And we were close and intimate and warm.

And we were stilled and captive in the peace
That welled from silence and that held us free
To fathom love, to salvage and release
The rich deposit of our constancy.

This was our harvest time, our ripened years,
A fruitage formed and firmed of mutable skies
Now warmed with joy, now watered deep with tears.
(Too swift, alas, the frost!) Our autumn dies.

We stirred and eased our clasp; I slowly rose,
Flicked on the light and sparked your cigarette.
You smiled: "Let's have some music; yours to choose."
I set the record of a Brahms quartet,

While you stood up to fetch your sewing box,
Then settled down domestically to heal
The laundry's wounds. The task of mending socks
For you was neither boredom nor ordeal.

Whether to build a fire, broil a steak,
Arrange a bowl of peonies, restore
A frazzled cushion or a cracked antique,
You were at home with each familiar chore.

I poked the embers, fed the struggling flare,
Our talk ran on—promise of years to come,
My poems to be, your classes on the Square,
Or gaily sailing to Byzantium.

We were there, completely together, close and sure,
Single in feeling, one in flavor and grain,
Rapt in an exquisite, rarefied aura of pure
Lumination. Never to bless us again.

Midnight stole in and caught us by surprise.
We roused ourselves to take a look at the weather;
We stepped into the deep outdoors; the skies
Loomed clean and crisp, the stars sang together.

Aglow, we sauntered back. I locked the door,
Snapped on the upstairs light. "Good night!" . . . "Sleep well!"
Your farewell country slumber. Nevermore
The country joys, the home you loved so well.

An Antique Dealer Drops By

The car slowed down,
Eased off the highway,
Turned into the driveway,
Threaded hidden behind the trees,
Curved, and gently halted
In the open, toward the house.

It didn't look like any friend's or neighbor's.
It was a black car,
A bulgy limousine,
The front seat for people,
The back for carting,
Ample as a hearse.

I wondered as the man stepped out
Whether he'd lost his way and needed direction,
Or what new gadget he hoped to trap me with.

"Good afternoon, sir:
May I introduce myself?"
I knew 'twas business before I'd read his card.

Walter Brackett,
Authentic Antiques,
Bristol, Connecticut.

"Authentic antiques,"
I pondered, over the card,
"That fits me to a T,
Provided, of course, four score and three
Will qualify."
The humor, if you'd call it that, escaped him.

To cut him off before he'd start his spiel,
I plumped out:
"You're wasting time on me. I'm not a prospect.
Whatever's here will have to do for a spell."

"I haven't come to sell; the car is empty,"
He countered with, "and waiting to be loaded.
You've got me wrong, I'm figuring to buy.

"I'd pay good money for a piece or so
I might be interested in. You see,
I know your things, I'm not a stranger here.
Three summers back, it's surely that by now,
I dropped around. Your missus came to the door,
Was kind to show me in. I well remember
The curly-maple beds, the piecrust table,
The walnut highboy and the wing chair
She picked up at a bargain, so she said,
While on a scouting jaunt up Ipswich way.
Right proud she was of all those lucky finds,
And with good reason, too; she sure had taste."

He hesitated, ventured on, and added:
"It must be lonesome now, with her away."

Shyly he paused, uncertain.
Commercialism had faded from his voice.
His sympathy was genuine, I felt,
Like that of an old friend.

I welcomed him, not in the hope of any
Spiritual food he might provide,
But rather as a sounding board. I'd kept
Within myself too long; I stood in need
Of simple conversation back and forth,
A chance to breathe more freely.

It's easier to loose one's tongue with a stranger
Passing by, not apt to meet again,
Than someone you feel close to. So I found
Myself replying:

"Lonesome, of course, at times, but not alone.
There's quite a difference there.

She's still about in every part of the place,
In every room of the house, and down below
In the garden, too; working on hands and knees
She set the plants to blossom with the seasons.
Each spring they're up again in all their colors—
Her legacy of beauty you might call it.

"Lover of beauty, that might best describe her,
In life as well as art. You should have seen
The state this place was in, a run-down wreck,
When we first came. It posed the sort of problem
That always challenged her imagination:
How to transform chaos into order.
That, I suppose, is what an artist's meant for;
In fact, that's what he lives for.

"And what she lived for, too.
                              Even if you missed
Her paintings on the walls, didn't you feel?—
You couldn't help but feel—you're not just business,
The artist in the color harmonies,
The gift that knew each object's proper setting,
The spirit that created this, a home?"

He turned to answer:
"I've not the words to tell it as you put it,
But still remember how I carried away
The picture this was what a home should be like.
I've found but few to match it."

And I went on:
"You've got me talking more than I had a mind to.
You stopped by here to trade and not to learn
What personally goes on in a man's heart.
Too bad you're out of luck for, when you leave,
You'll leave no better off than when you came.

"Yes,
I'm out of the market now and once for all.
What's here will stay so long as I'll be staying.

To sell off what she dearly brought together
Would be to strip a work of art, to scrap
A labor of love."

He rose and gripped my hand, then walked to the car.

"Come back," I called, "but don't be in a hurry."
He smiled and waved good-bye.

A Song for Linda

Linda lives in the welkin,
Linda, ten months old,
Snug in a snowy cloud cocoon,
Dreaming her warm, sweet milk in.

In Linda's vault of heaven
There's neither time nor space,
Neither morn nor even,
Only blessèd grace.

All innocence, she babbles
Her syllables of bliss,
In fragrant airs she dabbles
Within her chrysalis.

Within her microcosm,
So far, so high, so rare,
No evil leaps the chasm
From our polluted star.

Linda, there in the welkin,
Coos in her snug cocoon—
Her safe cocoon, and silken,
Dreaming her milk in.

David

David, finding adult speech
Quite beyond his infant reach,
Undismayed and resolute,
Seeks a working substitute.
David tests his vocal chords
On a language without words.

Hear his songs of innocence
Unimpaired by mood or tense,
Born of babbled syllables,
Treble notes and trillables.
In a music all his own
He converses all alone.

Imagination

At the age of three,
Lacking experience,
Common sense,
Even a scintilla of biology,
I planted chicken feathers in the snow.

Having seen flowers grow,
I took it for granted
That anything planted
Would turn out equally so.

How was I to know
The peculiar need
For suitable seed?

The Wading-Pool

Not content with the course it ran,
Favoring, rather, a personal plan,
The boy within me undertook
To tamper with the bed of a brook.

Better to cope with slippery rocks
I shed the clogs of shoes and socks;
Trouserless and bare of shank
I picked my steps on the tangled bank,

And where the shore-line turned a curve
Found an agreeable spot to serve,—
Quite the suitable site to fool
And fashion into a wading-pool.

Moss and fern and forest-rot
Twinkled with bright forget-me-not,
Maples, generous with shade,
Wove a leafy barricade.

Starting out in ooze and mud
That marked the sweep of April's flood,
I stooped and scooped until I found
A sweeter base of sandier ground,—

A deeper, cleaner, worthier base.
At last I'd decently cleared the place,
And, satisfied with all my clearing,
Now felt ready for engineering.

This was the problem straight at hand:
To pile up water, atop of sand,
Coax it over, give it shape,
Bar all openings of escape,—

All except an occasional slit
To keep the current pure and fit
To filter scum, alert to gather
And brew a froth of stagnant lather.

Out beyond, where a likely bend
Offered a definite usable trend,
I chose a rill for a leading runway,
Not too set on hurrying *one* way.

Not too bent on the way it went
It soon surrendered to argument,
Bade farewell to the main-line highway,
Then detoured and followed *my* way,

Loosening for easy travel
A lode of finely sifted gravel.
Here was a carpet firm and meet
To tempt the most reluctant feet.

Something nudged me, under foot,
Flowing water won't stay put;
It takes a curb to check its will.
It challenged me to haul and fill,—

Challenged me to stem the course
Of element, of wayward force,
Master nature, wrench from stone
World I could proclaim my own.

Hands are the most resourceful tools
For building-projects such as pools.
Still, by way of parenthesis,
A crowbar wouldn't have come amiss.

Eagerly I tugged and lugged,
Chose, discarded, planted, plugged,
Propped and calked,—the hollow filled,
Water rose. Water held!

Boldly hopping down the path,
A robin took the initial bath,
A testing, dedicating swim.
He praised the work. I followed him.

Snow Toward Evening

I have chosen "Snow Toward Evening" as the title of this book since it has been my most popular poem and is still being reprinted around the world. Moreover, it had the special distinction of being accepted for publication by Marianne Moore, the editor of the Dial, *in 1925.*

Suddenly the sky turned gray,
The day,
Which had been bitter and chill,
Grew soft and still.
Quietly
From some invisible blossoming tree
Millions of petals, cool and white,
Drifted and blew,
Lifted and flew,
Fell with the falling night.

Presence of Snow

So rare, so mere,
You cannot hear
It brush against the stillness or impair
With faintest stir
The poised, suspended air.

So rare, so mere,
And yet imponderably clear;
You cannot see, yet see
The secret flow
Of immanent snow,
Although
The softest breath has yet to free,
The gentlest current yet to take
The first bewildered flake.

Enchanted Snow

Now as I stand
Before the window and attend
The sailing, flurrying flakes, the whitening land,
I seek again in vain some clue or key
To liberate the guarded mystery.

This much, no more, I know:
That science, fixed to finite laws,
Is helpless to unveil
The supervening cause.
And so, once more, I fail.

Now, in my eighth decade, no wiser now
Than the spellbound child
Who first beheld, beguiled,
Long seventy years ago,
Enchanted snow.

Tawn Before Green

Far earlier than green,
It is the tawn
Steals in
To color April's dawn.

Tawn before green.

Delicately the willows
Array, with wealth of yellows,
The heartening scene,—
Tans, russets,
Saffrons, mustards,
And rare gold within,—

Tawn before green.

Summer Thunder

Broken into chunks
Of sound, like trunks
  drunkenly
    careering
      headlong
       down
         a stairway.

Clearing
The electric airway

Beginning to Rain

It seemed the first sharp spatter of rain
But only sound dripped from the branches.
Yet I'm not sure—
It may have been a warning of undropped drops,
Sent ahead
To get the leaves used to it.

One by One

One by one,
Branch to branch,
Leaves topple,
Zigzag
Through motionless October,
Struggle,
Founder;—
Golden birds
With broken wings.

Fine Rain

Fine rain
Drills with steel
Through ice;

Strings silver berries
On black branches;

Weaves sky
With sod.

Fog, the Magician

Wrapped in a cloak
Of gray mystery,
Fog, the magician,
Steals tip-toe out of the sea.
In seven-league boots
He skims across the sky,
Blowing out the sun,
Blotting out the blue.
On cobweb wires he slides to earth,
Glides through gardens surreptitiously
And sponges every color out of flowers.
Churches, houses, trees,
He wipes like chalky outlines from a slate.

Fog says: "Presto!"
And birds turn into nothing as they fly,
Men grow vague and vanish.
Fog lifts his hands!
And motor-cars roll off into a void,
Dogs evaporate,
Cats dissolve to bodiless meows.

Noiselessly, peacefully,
The old world ends.
Nothing remains
But fog and me
And another world to be.
Slowly, dimly,
I seem to feel
A little of the wonder and the joy
That must have gladdened God in the beginning,
Creation before him.

Bees, After Rain

Dormant, their house sodden with rain,
Stunned by sudden sun,
The bees stir, revive,
Charge wildly out of the hive,
Race
Furiously,
Then gloriously
Interlace
A golden skein.

Casually

I was lying on the grass,
Thinking of nothing in particular,
When a maple-leaf settled beside me
And laughed in the friendliest fashion.
You have no idea
What a pleasant hour we spent together.

Coast Headland

Deep below,
Skiffs
Dancing in dazzle.
High on piny cliffs,
Whiffs
Of wild rose,
Sniffs
Of salt.

Lying in Grass

August . . .
In high, dry grass.
Arm crooked,
Head cupped,
Ear sunk,
Flank pressed
Into earth.
Eyes are
Two field-mice,
Scurrying, scurrying
Through grass-tips
Sniffing shadows,
Nibbling sun-glints,
Darting back
Into sleep holes.

Engadine

In the high hills,
In the hollows of the high Swiss hills,
Far above the lake that sleeps
So still, so far below,
Lies an airier pool.
Its springs arise in fragrant space
Above the wild flowers,
And not a stream that flows therein
Flows through earth.
Across uneven pastures,
By the shores of the high pool,
Lumbering cows munch bright color,
Trample on fragrance.
From heavy throats of ever-hungry cows
Soft bells dangle;
Cows amble,
And sound runs and ripples from the bells,
Filling the pool.
Gay and sunny are the waters of sound.

In Alpine hills
A pool is fed by bells.

Somewhere Hid in the Wild

Now in the mid-day glare
The heavy valley drowses;
Only the lazy stir
Of chimney-smoke from houses.

Across the listless fields
A single cow-bell drones;
Step for step it yields
Its crumpled monotones.

Somewhere hid in the wild
An ever-unsatisfied bleat,
Like a feverish tenement child
Above an August street.

Once, at Tarascon

Once, at Tarascon,
I saw a flock of sheep
Filling an ancient lane.
Sunset dyed their fleece with mauve.
Startled,
They bunched and huddled,
And panic ran along their backs
Like quicksilver.

Frail Light

When streets are mounds of frozen mud
And the blood
Beats slow,
And above the town
The sky sags damp and brown,
And the raw February ebb
Carries the threat of snow, more snow,—
Through the steaming opaque mass
Frail lemon light may pass
And pierce the thickest vapors
That shroud skyscrapers,
And make a warm aërial alley,
So that the mind may sniff
The most faint and fleeting whiff,—
Arbutus trailing across an awakening valley.

Too Deleble, Alas!

Now that the sun has passed
Beneath the west,
Now that the rosy spread
Begins to fade
And after-light is thinning,
Night advances, winning
Inch on golden inch.
Too deleble, alas!
The dapple on the branch,
The shimmer on the grass;
The yellow-green too frail
On apple-leaves that pale.
Violet dims, night hastens,
Blue lessens, black fastens;—
Not a thing the eye shapes
Escapes.

Hail to the Major

On his gift of trees to surround St. Patrick's Cathedral. 1946

All hail to Major Edward Bowes,
Supreme of impresarios,
Who, magically, without theatrics,
Has set a grove around St. Patrick's,
Mightiest feat of legerdemain
Since Birnam moved to Dunsinane.
The ancient stones, austere and papal,
He warms with greenery of maple,
Building isles of cloistered shade
For office boy, for man and maid.

But is the major's appetite
For nature satisfied? Not quite.
He looks at John D. Junior's realm
Where elm sedately nods to elm,
Then plants his own, to parallel 'm.

And so, municipal thanks we give.
(We hope they'll live.)

To a Woman in a Bus, Embroidering an Initial

Impervious to jolt and halt,
To jarring lurch and rude assault,
Oblivious of shock and jerk
She prosecutes her needlework,
Prolongs the distaff rites of home,
The bus her second living room.

The world outside, the office day
Nonexistent miles away.

Across her lap the napkin's spread
To draw and hold the silken thread
And build the form and proudly frame
The precious emblem of her name.

From a Deck Chair

Whenever the steamer dips
Within its careening ellipse
It leans on the slope of the sea,
The sliding hill of the sea.

Whenever the steamer lifts,
The hillside flattens and shifts,
Descends and drags a sail
Down with it under the rail.

Park Pigeons

Still blue stones,
Dull gray rocks,
Sunk in grass.
A child flings a peanut.
Stones flutter,
Rocks circle in the sun.

New Yorkers

Boobs
Who mole in tubes
And mate in cubes.

H. & B.

Huntley
Utters
The news
More bluntly
Than Brinkley.

Brinkley
Twitters
And coos
More twinkly.

News

This blue-frost day
A feather
Lost in shining weather
Floats through a cloud,
Slips down a chimney.

The papers refuse
To report the news.
They'd sooner say
(And tuck it away):
"11:05 A.M.,
Moon sets."

Natural History Notes

I

The cobra
Is more vicious than the zebra,
Especially under Libra,
And all through Octobra.

II

The cougar
Is fierce,
The tiger
Is worse.
So don't be too eager
To woo them with sugar,
When feeding them sugar
Be wary, be meager.

III

The puma
Is socially non grata to the llama
And has been since the days of Montezuma.
Its personal aroma
Is rank enough to sink one in a coma.
You'll not find either beast in Alabama
Or Oklahoma.

IV

The anaconda
Bears not the least resemblance to the panda.
The panda,
When trained, is safe to keep on your veranda.
But, as the natives warn in far Uganda,
Never, never trust an anaconda.

The Mussel

The mussel,
While to outward view a fossil,
Is very much alive inside.
His pride
Is quite colossal;
He's snobbishly selective
And shuts him in his shell the more protectively
To guard his privacy against intrusion.
His torpor is a snare and a delusion.

The Ea-gull

The Ea-gull
(Bald,
So-called)
Bulks far bigger
Than the Sea-gull.
He cuts a figger
Monumental, rea-gull.

It would be less than lea-gull
To invea-gull
An unassuming sea-gull
For a contest with an ea-gull.
He isn't in the same league with an ea-gull.

And neither is a bea-gull.

Diffidence

I never seek a combat
With a wombat;
A foray
From a moray
I would shun.
The mildest kind of tussle
With a jellyfish or mussel
Is not my notion of fun.

I never pick a quarrel
With a squirrel,
A creature
Whose ill-nature
I suspect;
While a rough-and-tumble battle
With an up-and-coming rattler
I would utterly, emphatically reject
And eschew.

Wouldn't you?

Luck

The mastodon and dinosaur
Are absolutely obsolete.
The moa, roc, with all their stock,
Are now, distinctly, quite extinct.
But why repine and why deplore
What Nature chooses to delete?
We might have been, sans kith or kin,
Irrevocably missing-linked.

On Shabby Green

In early April
On shabby green
Nervous robins pivot, balance,
Curve, dash, curve, dash,
Bill up, tail down,
Bill down, tail up.

Into shabby green
Thrusting robins peck!
Out of shabby green
Tugging robins pluck
Little lively things,
Things that dart and wriggle.

Fat and sated robins
Saunter and meander,
Loiter as they wander
Under bursting maples,
Over rugs of ruddy buds
Blown on shabby green.

Meadow Incident

The hound-dog
Chased the ground-hog
Into its hole,
Frantically scraped the dirt away at the top,
Finally came to a stop,
Defeated
And considerably overheated.

Barking a crestfallen cough
Or two, the hound-dog trotted off
And soon was busily pawing the track of a mole.

Warily
The ground-hog poked out
Its snout,
Airily
Drew a relieved sniff
And a scornful whiff,
Then waddled across the succulent field to scrunch
A crisp, low-calorie lunch.

Flash!

Skip of chipmunk;
Spring of frog;
Swoop of hawk;
Strike
Of snake;
Leap of dog;
Dart of trout;
Cat-pounce!—

Flashes! born
Of body-scorn,
Dashing, dashing out,—
Unbound
To ounce
Or pound.

The Woodchuck

On the Fourth of last July,
After a substantial breakfast,
I was seated on the porch
In a comfortable chair,
Skimming the news
And casually inviting the Muse.

The morning opened bright and fair
And in the bland congenial air
I felt agreeably relaxed,
The mind untaxed,
Without concern or care.

The world looked good, I was half inclined
To think the better of humankind,
When suddenly, to break the spell,
My eyes fell
Upon a woodchuck boldly on the lawn.

Now, had the creature chanced to be a fawn,
Or, happily, a unicorn,
I should have embraced it joyfully and sworn
Eternal comradeship, but this intruder,
Marauder
And despoiler of my garden,
Hardened the heart and kindled a lust for murder.

Such was the swift response, and yet, the will
To action failed;
A deeper sense prevailed,
Commanded and enjoined: "Thou shalt not kill!"

Then I saw the 'chuck with a juster eye
And a lighter mood;
I remembered it was the Fourth of July,
And if *I* was free,
Then, why not *he?*

Not bent on crime or out for food,
He was simply taking a holiday stroll
For a change of scene from his hole
In the field
And the nervous strain of keeping concealed.

He had chosen, instead, an innocent way
To celebrate Independence Day,
With the same inalienable delights
As anyone under the Bill of Rights.

Emily Dickinson

Enclosed within a hedge
Of hemlock, doubts and nays,
A burning spinster paced
Her clipped New England days.

While pretty singers droned
A local, nasal hymn,
She raised a timeless voice;
It reached the spatial rim.

She never saw a moor,
She never saw the sea,
Yet from a hilltop in her heart
She scanned Infinity.

Hokinson

Her subject Womankind, her special model
The dowager in danger of a waddle,
That matron of a fairly ripe and round age
Whose inausterity pays off in poundage.

Hers was the art that launched a thousand hips
And firmly tucked the bulge beneath the girdle,
That picked those silly hats on shopping trips,
Those foolish frocks that scaled the social hurdle.

And hers the wit to catch the fatuous unction
Of Madam Chairman at some garden function,
And register the embarrassing inanities
Of females, willing victims of their vanities.

Her pencil, poised in mischief, camera-candid,
Scored cleaner hits than ever any man did,
And gentler, too, the satire and the mockery
More kind than Swift, more frolicsome than Thackeray,
As if to say: "One never can be tellin';
Yes, there, but for the grace of God, goes Helen."

To W. W.

Let's not debate in whom the fault,
The melancholy fact is, Walt,
That I can take your rhapsodies
In ever diminishing quantities.
Yes, let it once for all be stated,
I disincline to your inflated
Rhetoric, your chant verbose,
Oh! Maestro of the grandiose!

Oh! Singer of the Cosmic Whole,
Despite your lack of self-control
I gladly praise your reach of soul.
When fashioning a universe
One can't, I freely grant, be terse,
But why do you have to say it twice,
When once, by being more concise,
Were doubly more than twice effective?

Oh! had you learned to be selective,
My camerado!—less *en masse*—
And cleared those lusty leaves of grass
Of all those heaves of gusty gas!

Mr. Eliot's Cat Book

"Mr. T. S. Eliot's intimate friends receive from time to time type-written verses which are apparently anonymous but which are always identifiable. The poems, which concern cats, are presented here."
—Publisher's blurb.

When T. S. Eliot stoops to folly,—
A circumstance to marvel at,—
He bids adieu to melancholy
And lightly turns to thoughts of cat.

And lightly turns a nimble ballad
In praise of Thomas or of Tab,
With here and there a hint, though valid,
Of something else by Lear or "Bab."

To poetize the genus feline
And please alike adults and chil'n,
He swings a wide, elastic free-line
Which makes one think at times of Milne.

When T. S. Eliot sips his malmsey
And mulls and mellows by the grate,
He now and then succumbs to whimsey,
A weakness one must deprecate.

After Reading the Reviews of "Finnegans Wake"

Nothing has been quite the same
Since I heard your liquid name,
Since it cast a magic spell,
Anna Livia Plurabelle.

Maid or river, bird or beast,
Doesn't matter in the least,
Quite enough that tongue can tell
Anna Livia Plurabelle.

What you've done, you'll never guess,
To my stream of consciousness!
Hang the meaning! What the hell!
Anna Livia Plurabelle.

E. E. Cummings

Although he chose to sing in lower-case,
A whim, perhaps,
Posterity will reset the type, and place
His name in CAPS.

Lady-Poet (Of Either Sex)

She loves to whittle
And shave her feelings
And save the peelings
Pretty and brittle;

Enjoys the titil-
lation and subtle
Play of verbal
Shuttle and burble;

Toys with mystic
Rapture and terror—
All in a narcissistic
Mirror.

A Thurber Carnival

The face
Deadpan,
The voice
Deadsober,
The treatment,
The texture,
A tricky mixture
Of overtones and understatement.

You're at the entry
Of a bewildering country.
Here,
There's much of import to impart
And more than meets the callous ear.

Observe the horse *behind* the cart,
Absorb the shocks
Of paradox.

Discover the uncommon sense
That lurks around irrelevance,
And witness man's fatuity
When shackled to congruity;

And chuckle at the irony
That salts the human comedy,
And revel in that airy land,
That daffy, quite-contrary land,
Where Thurber's sly executors
Unreel their mad non sequiturs.

The Author Retrieves a Presentation Copy of His Book

Upon a dingy sidewalk stall,
Exposed to city rain and grime,
I found it, marked for burial,
Though priced at but a dime.

Indeed it were indignity
To stuff it in a pauper's grave,
But who might venture, saving me,
To rescue and reprieve?

I paid the ransom, clasped the waif
With all the warmth of parentage,
And as I held it, close and safe,
I turned the title page,

And—sore humiliation—read
The words of gift I once had penned
For one whom I had credited
And cherished as a friend.

I might have borne his perfidy
And nursed my wounds in silence, but
For this supreme effrontery,
The pages were uncut.

Orchestra Notes

Pity the wretched harp-player!
Lord, he must suffer a pang or two,
Sitting up there
For the whole of a symphony,
Plucking no more than a twang or two.

Pity the hapless drummer!
What man's lot could be glummer?
Tense with concern,
Waiting his turn
To release his appropriate bang or two.

And the scrupulous wielder of cymbals,
On pins and needles and thimbles!
Marking each beat
For the moment discreet
To crash his climacteric zing or two.
(*He* surely could tell us a thing or two.)

But what, if anyone misses?
Who gets the hisses, the odium?
Would anyone choose
To step into the shoes
Of the guy on the brink of the podium?

Bed-Time Story

Once there was a spaniel
By the name of Daniel,
And a pig,
Sig,
And a pussy,
Gussie,—
She chased a mouse,
Klaus;
And a squirrel,
Errol,
And a white she-bear,
Claire,
And a Scotch lion,
Ian,
And a very fierce shark,
Mark.

You'll agree, my dear,
They were rather a queer
Assortment
Of temperament and deportment.

And yet,
My pet,
In spite of their diversities
And perversities
Both zoological
And ideological,
They all gathered together
One day, when the weather
Was especially frightful, and decided
It wasn't safe to stay divided
Any longer, and that they should,
For their common good,
(Rather than risk another calamity)
Try amity.

And that's the way there began to dawn a
Plan they christened UNITED FAUNA.

. . .

"And did they live happily ever after, daddy?"
"I'll tell you the rest tomorrow. Good-night, dear."

Operatic Note

Apparently the Nibelungs
Were never cursed with feeble lungs.

The World Around Us

Folks in Fordham
Die of bordham.

In Canajoharie
They just won't marie.

But in Yonkers
Love conkers.

These nights, at Cazenovia,
You sleep with blankets ovia.

Some move to Oneonta,
Others don't wonta.

Throughout the whole of China
There's not an Elk or Shrina.

And, likewise, in Canarsie,
One seldom meets a Parsee.

It's blackberry time at Pelham.
They can 'em, stew 'em, jelham.

The summer crowd at Brewster
Is bigger than it yewster.

A nudist fan at Hudson
Was warned to put his dudson

A physicist at Chatham
Last Monday split an atham.

Lines After a Motor Trip
Through the South

George Washington,
Parens Patriae;
Robert E. Lee,
"That my men may retain their horses";
Patrick Henry,
"Or give me death";
Thomas Jefferson,
"When, in the course of";
Stonewall Jackson,
"Dies like a dog";—
March on, march on!
Your shining names with us shall ever dwell,
Fixed to a first- or possibly second-
Rate hotel.

Punctuation Note

(*a clerihew*) *

Wise old Solon
Eschewed the colon;
However, Saint Thomas
Was lavish with commas.

* *Clerihew: a satiric or comic poem, usually in two couplets. After Edmund Clerihew Bentley, 1875–1956, English novelist.*

1770-1831

George Wilhelm Friedrich Hegel
Simply couldn't abide the bagel;
His favorite bread,
Instead,
(And often with a mustard pickle)
Was pumpernickel.

It Isn't

It isn't the heat;
It's the humidity.
It isn't the cold;
It's the frigidity.
It isn't the bulk;
It's the solidity.
It isn't the grief;
It's the morbidity.

It isn't the speed;
It's the rapidity.
It isn't the greed;
It's the avidity.
It isn't the thaw;
It's the liquidity.
It isn't the law;
It's the juridity.

It isn't the vice;
It's the perfidity.
It isn't the ice;
It's the too-skidity.
It isn't the glue;
It's the viscidity.
It's not even you;
It's my hyperacidity.

Ornithological

The shriek of a shrike
I dislike;
The look of a rook
I can't brook;
The wail of a quail
I'd curtail;
The squeal of a teal
Lacks appeal;
The lilt of a stilt
Best unspilt;
The gush of a thrush
Pure mush;
The hoot of a coot
Leaves me mute,
And I'm immune
To the croon of a loon.

As for nightingales and curlews,
Glad they don't infest these purlieus.

Let's Behoove

"This diplomatic penetration of Latin America by Moscow is not necessarily bad, or alarming. But it would seem to behoove the United States to keep in good repair its own diplomatic fences."
                                                            —New York Times *Editorial.*

Though there may be no harm
In this Soviet move,
And no cause for alarm
And no ground for distress,
Still, nevertheless,
It would seem to behoove,
It's the obvious time to behoove us.

Though the Gaucho and Russ
Seek legitimate trade,
And their posture toward us
Be as pure as the dove,
Yet, it can't be gainsaid,
It would seem to behoove
That the moment's at hand to behoove us.

Though we far from suspect
Any mischievous scheme,
And we fail to detect
Any evidence grave,
Just in case—it would seem
(Though of course they'll behave)
That we'd better begin to behoove us.

Cows

Cows have such a serious look,
They must be thinking.
But I don't know—
I've seen
The same look
On men.

Spots and Stripes

The leopard, uncomplaining of his lot,
Is disinclined to change a single spot—
Quite sensibly, the leopard wouldn't,
Because he knows he couldn't.

The zebra, though condemned to prison-stripes,
Is philosophical and never gripes.

But man, rebellious and tormented biped,
Grapples with fate, unspotted and unstripéd.

Incurably

Though it prove idle, yet I seek
Incurably, and dream of the peak,
Knowing well my farthest hope
Were but a footing along the slope.

A Snatch, at Least

The sea drinks up
The sand.
I saunter along the strand
And note a retreating wave.
I kneel
And, as I kneel,
I hastily make of my hand
A cup,
A sieve,
With which to wrest and retrieve
And, wryly, save
From the sea's command
A snatch, at least, of land.

By One, Unsure

My feet toe in, as Indians' do,
A natural gait,
And as I track across the snow,
Pursuing fate,
My thoughts turn inward, shutting out
The world's distractions roundabout.

I pause a step and gaze behind
To note a pattern well-defined,
Stampings from a special mint
As personal as fingerprint.

The course between, a winding path
Of strait and unassuming breadth,
By one, unsure of destinies,
Who swerves within parentheses.

Honey

This tilted jar
Urges amber flow;
Ambrosial
Material,
Thick stuff, loath
And slow
To yield its sloth
And grudgingly transmute
Its liquid attribute.

Two elements at war;
Glacier in miniature.

Triad

Memory goes, with age;
Print lies dim on the page;
Snowflakes melt upon the window ledge.

A Candle

A candle is a thing of wax
Whose life presents a paradox:
When little more than wick remains
It blithely waxes as it wanes.

Newborn

Loosed from the womb,
Thrust rudely into April,
Stunned by the sun,
They blink, they bleat, bewildered
By this other-world—
Newborn lambs
A-wobble on new-found limbs.

Squirrels

Tightrope or slack wire,
These specialists in higher acrobatics
Move equally and easily at home.
Prime stars in Nature's vaudeville,
They rate the topmost billing.

I watch them chase each other
Through the bare elms,
And race together
For no apparent end or reason
Except the need of exercise
Against the season's chilling.

Master equilibrists,
They match their weight
To the give of the branch,
The yield of the bough,
The sag of the quivering twig,

And, in conclusion,
As if to prove that they are pros,
They end their act
With a furious flourish of tails
In a shameless bid for applause.

They know not how to fail;
They never fall.

Notwithstanding, Nevertheless

This poem has had an unusual history. It was born in 1935, rejected by Harper's Magazine, *and then lost to both sight and memory. It was only when gathering the material for* All and Sundry *that I rediscovered it, no worse for its long interment. At least such was the judgment of the editor of the* Atlantic Monthly, *where it appeared in the February, 1968, issue.*

Lady that I've taken to
(Why?—I can't awaken to),
How you hold my fond attention
Circumvents my comprehension.
I might mention, what you give
Out is largely negative.
Yet, you start a tender current
I'd be missing if it weren't.
I can only dimly guess
You've a something, nevertheless,
Yes, a downright nevertheless.

Lady, I'm as flatly baffled
As a whale upon a scaffold.
You are pitiably plain,
Your ensemble's unattractive,
Your apology-for-brain
Is congenitally inactive;
Though you lack and though I miss
All the charms I'm most demanding,
Still you compensate with this:
You've a potent notwithstanding,
Yes, a yet and notwithstanding.

Hear a victim in distress,
Nevertheless and notwithstanding;
Heal a fever that's expanding
Notwithstanding, nevertheless.

Meet the Middles

I sing an American family
Equally important as the Cabots,
Vanderbilts,
Or even the Philadelphia Biddles,
And notable
As a tribe
Of quotable
Scribes—
In short, the Middles.

Chief among those
Who function
With distinction
Are:
William Middle Bryant,
Henry Middle Longfellow,
John Middle Whittier,
James Middle Lowell,
Oliver Middle Holmes.

They're skilled in prose
And apt with poems
(Including Holmes).

And quite as admirable as they
Is Edna St. Middle Millay.

Eloquent April

April, awakening
hour, the word itself a quickening!

Take the initial *A,* open
and eager to call in
the fresh aerial currents of the North.

Then, *p, r,* tools to pry and prod
the stubborn sod
and warm it to rebirth.

Finally, *i* and *l,*
liquid, lyrical
to the tongue,
high-charged with promises of song
and spring!

April, sign of Aries,
Arise!

Strategy

To mingle along, as one in the midst,
To seem a part, yet hold apart,
To build a shield, with bewildering art,
To outwit, and persist.

Consider the Flowers

Consider the flowers;
their lives as dear as ours.
Tread not upon a trillium;
be tender with sweet william.

* * *

Dust are Thebes and Ilium.

The Designation

I caught it, as it floated by,
a solitary, vagrant word,
quite innocent of destiny.

I sought it, begging no reward,
'twas Chance, alone, who ordered it,
and Chance, it was, who singled me
to guard the seed within the word,
to feed the song within the seed.

To the Aging

. . . Both as lawyer and poet you evidently realize that the feeling for words leads to comparison, contrast and choice, the basis of intelligence and true knowledge. And it has even led you to the frontiers of the kingdom of chance—the source and origin of creative opportunity, without which history would be truly monotonous and evolution run down.—Letter of William King Gregory, July 12, 1953.

Treasure the gift of choice,
(Man's vital
fuel!)
and still
care, still
be critical,
approve or disapprove,
despise or love.

Rejoice
in April's
renewal.

Keep open the gates of chance!

The Given Weapon

We're born,
and in that fateful instant of our birth
death too, along, is born.

We grow,
and with our gradual growth—
so negligent of danger!—
we harbor
unwittingly the foe.

Slow
to awaken and become aware,
we spot
the enemy at last,
deep in his unsuspected lair.

None too soon!
We bestir ourselves, hard driven
to discover
the ultimate strategy
and wield the given
weapon—
not one
useless in the usual field
of war

against unbearable odds,
but, rather, one
to disarm, dissemble, and outwit
by happier means:
equipment
from heaven's armament;
our natal grant
of the overseeing gods,
the heritage of innocence.

Two

Too heavy-footed
to fly,
he'll be rooted
to earth till he die.

Too airy, too light
to descend,
she'll spin out her flight
till the end.

So tied,
so buoyed
that neither
can lighten the lot of the other.

Time Enough for That

I'm sorry for all those who have agreed to grow old. I
haven't agreed yet.—E. B. White, New York Times, *July*
11, 1969.

I quite agree with White.

As far as blood incites,
as long as spirit burns,
I'll follow my concerns
as always, more or less,
with no especial stress
on what was once
or since,
or what may chance to be.

As long as I keep free
and sane, and sound of breath,
there'll be no truck with death,
I'll make no pact with death.

There's time enough, however late,
for that.

The Problem

"The problem from now on,"
observed the old man as he
looked out on the falling
flakes, "is how to prolong the
weathering without the withering?"

Obiters

To be in fashion
exude compassion.

*

To shine charismal
suppress the dismal.

*

Too much computer
will make men neuter.

*

To become a sage
takes more than age.

*

Humility:
ability
to relate one's ego
to the cosmos.

*

Candor
can be
simply bad manners.

*

Book title:
Poems, Few and Neglected.

*

"I stand for principle,"
he mouthed,
but really, for prejudice.

*

Modesty:
a technique of behavior,
not a virtue.

*

To pass as a humanitarian
one needn't be humane.

*

Before composing
become composed.

*

Cogitate,
else vegetate.

*

He's a reactionary,
to the very narrow of his bones.

*

"He's with I.B.M.,
computes from Westport."

*

"Your novel stirred me so deeply
I could hardly keep it down."

*

Quintus Trig,
professor of logic at Quantum University,
died today of a corollary.

*

Walt Whitman
might have developed
into a great poet
but for the influence of
Thomas Wolfe.

*

They swallow,
but fail to taste.

*

How difficult to curb
an active intransigent verb!

*

Never lie—
unnecessarily.

*

Alumnus:
His one ideal
is to preserve the infantile.

*

Her letters
are as diverting as
receipted bills.

*

To achieve
poetic longevity
weave
levity
with gravity.

*

"I value myself upon *this,*
that there is nothing
of the old man
in my conversation."
Dr. Johnson.

Thanks, Sam,
for the reminder.

*

Life would be more agreeable
were the future more foreseeable.

*

My life style
must do for a while.

*

Four Clerihews *

I
AERIAL

Percy Bysshe Shelley
Despised the telly.
"Nevertheless it certainly beats
The radio," contended Keats.

II
HISTORIC NOTE

Emperor Nero
Was no hero.
He yielded weakly to desire;
He shouldn't've fiddled with fire.

III
DOMESTIC SCENE

Browning, perched upon a log,
Polished off a monolog;
Lizzie, seated more at ease,
Sonneted from the Portuguese.

IV
LITERARY NOTE

Algernon Swinburne
Died of skin burn.
"Must have been tippling,"
Concluded Kipling.

* See note, p. 88.

Jabberdegook

Religiously, on bended knees,
I exercised my expertise;
With practiced and consummate ease
I split my twin identities.
I envied none their aperçus
But flattered them with tongue-in-cheek,
Then drew it back-the tongue-in place
In nick of time to save my face.

'Twas then I saw my proud mystique
Had sublimated, and that fate
Had lost its power to alienate
And left me free to integrate.

To My Poems

When I no longer chance to be
Enveloped in mortality
You'll still abide, the residue
Of all experience struggled through.
You still will hold, distilled, the essence
Of what was, once, a vital presence
Who strove, in song, to manifest
The pain, the joy, within the breast.

A Kind of Sound

I sit on a shaded porch,
inactively serene.
It's a hundred yards from the road;
a meadow's in between.
It's a soundless hour in June,
the random birds are still,
the sun is cordial and bland,
a book lies closed in the hand.

The faintest stir in the air
falls on a somnolent ear.
I'm not quite sure what I hear,
till it shapes, as it builds afar,
to the whir of a passing car.

Nightfall

Blue
thins.
Beige
dims.
Timidly,
out of the lilac hedge,
the first firefly
tentatively
tastes
and tests
the black.

Autumnal

These leaves, once filled with chlorophyl,
must soon submit to Nature's will,
and with the earliest deadly frost
their verdant color will be lost,
to be replaced by carotene
as well as anthocyanin.

In other words, more simply told:
Wake up some day and you'll behold
the maples, proud in rose and gold.

Changing Rooms

At the hospital
the invalid
moved
serenely,
philosophically,
from TERMINAL
to eternal
CARE.

Footnote to Genesis

Adam, when he parted
with a rib,
had no idea he'd started
Women's Lib.

*

They'll equal be,
with women in,
but will they lose
what's feminine?

The Little Boy

(After the return from Peking and Moscow)

The little boy
was shrewd and sly;
he always managed
to get by,
and after he
had risen high
and scanned the
advantageous sky,
he still pursued
his youthful game
and played it
pretty much the same,
and, finding the
old method worked,
he, smug with
satisfaction, smirked;
"How marvelously smart am I."

Obiters

Her weltanschauung
is cosmetic,
rather than
cosmic.

*

The atmosphere
of the current epoch
does not conduce
to produce
an epic.

*

In much of Dickens
bathos thickens.

*

The greater the speed
the smaller the space.

Editor

Ezra Pound,
knife in hand,
cut out the "Waste"
to save the "Land."

Tribute

A toast to E. C. Bentley, who
contrived with wit and aperçu
a four-line verse called Clerihew,*
(but mastered by a very few).

*See note, p. 88.

Parsonical

There once was an Anglican parson
who harbored a weakness for arson.

*

The reason
I mention
this person
is merely
to fashion
this verse on.

On Escaping a Mortal Illness

The Irresist-
ible Reaper,
eyes ashift,
missed
a tuft.

Index of Titles